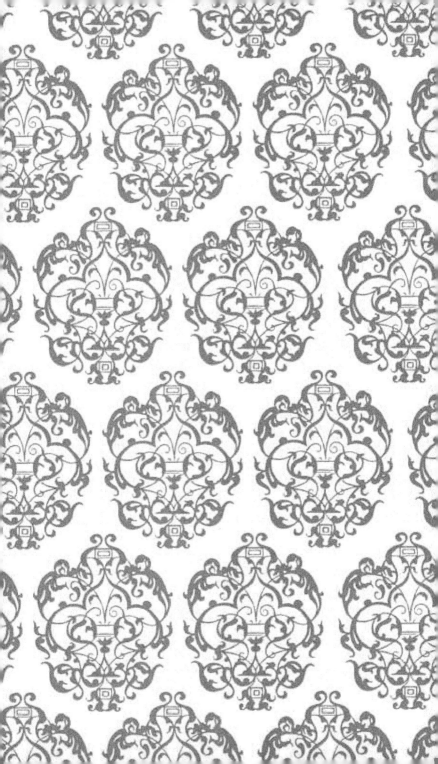

GROCERY
SHOPPING
WITH GOD

MAKING THE MUNDANE MEANINGFUL
THROUGH MITZVAHS

KAREN KUFLIK

Grocery Shopping With God
Copyright© 2012 by Karen Kuflik

Published by
Karen Kuflik

ISBN: 978-1-935110-16-3

Printed in the United States

DEDICATION

To my husband Mitchell, my own Moshe, who brought Torah
into our lives.

And to Manny, Nathan and Simon who bring Torah to life
every single day.

INTRODUCTION

Right now you are doing a mitzvah. Actually you are doing more than one. You are taking time out for yourself (mitzvah #1), you are learning Torah (mitzvah #2) and you are giving tzedekah as the proceeds from the book are going to charity (mitzvah #3). By the time you finish reading this book, you will probably discover that you are doing far more than the three mitzvahs I just mentioned. The idea for *Grocery Shopping with God* came directly from a series of lectures by Rebbetzin Esther Baila Schwarz, a brilliant, funny, warm teacher from Monsey, New York. I told her many times that her ideas would make a great book and she said, "Then write it!!" Little did she know that, actually, I am a writer by profession. But writing children's television and writing Jewish self-help books couldn't be more different. So after many years of percolation and procrastination, here it is.

The premise of this book is that in our daily routines, we are inherently doing mitzvahs. Every hour, every day, week in and week out, literally thousands and thousands of them. Whether we are driving carpool, going grocery shopping or cleaning out closets, these seemingly endless, rote activities can actually be mitzvahs! How can this be? Contrary to the popular notion that a mitzvah is a good deed, the actual definition of the word "mitzvah" is "commandment." A mitzvah is a commandment straight from God designed to give your life purpose and meaning. This book will examine mitzvahs from the Torah that we are already doing, (most likely without realizing it) and help us understand them better. This understanding will allow you to elevate the mundane to the meaningful, transforming the daily grind into a daily goldmine.

MY BACKGROUND

I was raised in a suburb of Buffalo, New York as a conservative Jew. I went to Hebrew school (begrudgingly). I had a Bat Mitzvah (pink and green were my colors ... long before today's elaborate themes). I even continued with confirmation classes post-bat-mitzvah. I went to Jewish sleep away camp in Canada. I was one of two or three Jews in my class at public school. I had a strong Jewish identity and even a healthy amount of Torah knowledge (one year even making it to the finals of the county bible contest!). But I had no clue about God.

I went to college. Dated a non-Jew (or two). Drove my parents crazy. Moved to New York City. Dated another non-Jew. Then I met my husband on a blind date. He was an unaffiliated Jew, but he was a Jew nonetheless (congregation shouts "Amen!"). And a wonderful, wandering, searching Jew at that, a man who, through a series of events and circumstances (there are no coincidences), brought me and my family much closer to God and Torah observance.

In terms of career, I was an advertising copywriter turned children's television writer turned infertility treatment mom-to-be freelancer turned mother of three beautiful boys (at one point all under two years of age!) When my boys began school full time, I found myself asking "*Now* what do I do?!?" "Do I need to work in order to feel fulfilled?" When someone at a party asks, "So what do you do?" my answer of being a mom, accompanied by a shoulder shrug felt hollow and unimportant. I was at a crossroads. I considered myself an accomplished, intelligent woman. But how could I find meaning in my seemingly mundane life?

For the first time, I began taking Torah based classes (that's how I met Esther Bayla who inspired this book!) which led to more classes some of which I went to all the way to Israel to take. The more I learned, the more I understood that Torah and Jewish wisdom have practical applications to improve everyday life.

One surprising theme that emerged was that I could have a personal relationship with God. Who knew? This journey has led me and my family to move houses, change schools and observe Shabbat and the holidays (yes, even Shemini Atzeret!). I am still very much a work in progress, in terms of observance and daily practice, but every Jew – even those born into ultra orthodox families– are works in progress, finding new and better ways to connect with each other and God.

I hope that this book can help any Jew at any level to elevate the mundane to the meaningful.

MITZVAHS 101

There are 613 mitzvahs* mentioned in the Torah – 248 positive commandments (the do's) and 365 negative ones (the don'ts). The great 12th century Jewish philosopher, Maimonides enumerated and categorized these mitzvahs in his famous work Sefer HaMitzvoth. Because the holy Temple in Jerusalem no longer stands, many of the mitzvahs that applied to Temple services cannot be practiced today. The 19th century Rabbi and scholar, the Chofetz Chayim, identified 77 positive and 194 negative mitzvahs which are still applicable to our lives. Many of these however pertain to people living in the land of Israel so that narrows it down further. This book will explore a small subset of "generic" practical mitzvahs that can be applied to our everyday lives.

1

In addition to the mitzvahs mentioned in the Torah, there are many other corollaries and offshoots which are also called mitzvahs in Judaism, providing us with additional opportunities to join God's team. (Indeed, this is the deeper meaning of the word "mitzvah," which shares its root with the word *litzvot*, meaning "to join," and with the word *tzevet* meaning "team.")

There are mitzvahs pertaining to family, friends, holidays, business dealings, food, legal matters, and even sex. There is basically a mitzvah for almost everything we do: from putting on a seat belt to not losing it when the "express" checkout is anything but. Our job is to figure out which mitzvah goes with which action and inject the requisite holiness into that seemingly mundane activity. The hope is by retrofitting mitzvahs into actions we are already doing, we will enhance and elevate our lives.

*I am aware that the proper plural word for mitzvahs is mitzvoth, but for the colloquial style of this book and its audience I am using the word "mitzvahs." Just had to clarify that.

TAKE CARE

"Guard yourself and guard your soul very much." Deuteronomy 4:9-10

The mitzvah of guarding your health is pivotal to all other mitzvahs. Try lighting Shabbat candles without a body! Or driving carpool! The mitzvah to take care of yourself has two sides: avoiding harmful risks and developing healthy habits. Now for some practical applications:

When you reach across and put on your seat belt (for the sixth time today), you are performing a mitzvah. The same goes for going to the gym, walking the dog, eating a salad for lunch and saying no to your third margarita. The trick is to stop, take a moment and realize that these simple acts are actually mitzvahs. It is very easy to rush through your day on autopilot. The next time you book a massage or take that afternoon nap, consider it a mitzvah! Obviously overdoing the hedonism is not a mitzvah, but taking good care of yourself gives you the best chance to fulfill all the other mitzvahs.

While we live in a very physical world in physical bodies with physical needs, remember the body houses the all important soul. Every physical action we take affects our soul. What we see and hear, what we do and say impacts us on a much deeper level than just the physical. God is commanding us to protect our bodies so our souls can have the best chance of fulfilling our potential here on earth.

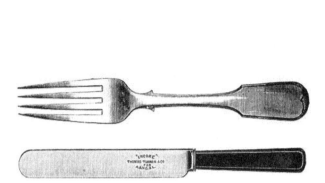

THINK BEFORE YOU EAT

"Do not eat or drink like a glutton." Deuteronomy 20:21

According to the Torah, another way to take care of the body is to eat and drink in moderation. Long before fad diets and flax seed, the Rambam wrote, *"One should not eat all that one desires like a dog or a donkey. Rather, one should eat what is beneficial for the body, be it bitter or sweet. Conversely, one should not eat what is harmful to the body, even though it is sweet to the taste."* Behold the original Weight Watchers. He went on to say *"One should not eat until one's stomach is full. Rather one should stop when one reaches close to three-quarters of being full."* When we eat or drink to excess (which is painfully easy to do) we are feeding the physical part of us and starving our souls. Eating healthy and taking care of our bodies is a mitzvah. Pass the kale, please!

The commandments of keeping kosher are another way to stop and think before we eat or drink something. A friend told the following story:

> *"Betty struggled for years with her weight. She finally found a program and stuck with it. The pounds fell off, and she felt and looked great. Then Betty was invited to a reception where she knew all her favorite fattening dairy desserts would be served. She was afraid that once she opened the sweet floodgates, she would revert back to her old eating habits and start gaining weight. She didn't think she had the will power to attend the event. But she had a brilliant idea. She told me that before she went out she ate a nice piece of chicken. Then, because of the kosher law of not eating dairy foods for several hours after a meat meal, she could safely attend with no question of breaking down. It was a breeze!"*

The non-negotiable nature of God's commandments is the ultimate "because I said so!" It can be a great tool to help us manage how we eat and what we eat.

Another food-related mitzvah is making a blessing before and after eating foods. This helps us be more mindful and grateful consumers. How often do we wolf something down while watching TV or talking on the phone? Where did that bag of chips go? Like many of God's commandments, making a blessing elevates the physical to the spiritual. It also reminds us who gave us the food in the first place.

If you are like most people (myself included) who did not grow up making blessings, this can be overwhelming because there are many different kinds of blessings for the different foods we eat. So start out making a blessing over one thing a day. For example, your morning coffee, or something you really enjoy. Even if you don't know Hebrew, you can thank God out loud any way that feels right to you. For example: "Thank you Hashem, my Creator, who gave me this delicious, hot, rich cup of coffee." So sipping your morning brew becomes a mitzvah. Isn't that a good way to start your day?

It is also a commandment to say grace or "bench" after you are done eating. And similarly there are different prayers for different foods eaten. It only takes a mindful minute at the end of the meal. And we all know how good it feels to have your food appreciated. Like making blessings before you eat, benching afterwards can be overwhelming. Again, try it once a day. My family started out benching Friday nights. The more times a day we can recognize and acknowledge God as the supreme Provider, the better off we'll be. So you can have your cake and eat it too (just don't forget the blessing!)

WHAT WOULD GOD DO?

"Emulate His ways." Deuteronomy 28:9

Another foundational mitzvah is to act like God. This may seem like a lofty longshot, but there are very hands-on, doable ways of emulating our Creator. For example, moms know the nighttime drill of picking up strewn shoes, packing up backpacks, making lunches, slipping forgotten homework into folders. This can be viewed as a thankless chore. But when reframed as a mitzvah, any chore can become a holy act. A mother is very much like God who gives to, sustains and cares about His beautiful children!

When you go to the grocery store and pick out three different kinds of yogurt for your kids and husband, you are emulating God. How? God is constantly giving each of us exactly what we need. You are doing the same thing.

Moms often feel like short-order cooks in the kitchen. (This one wants his bagel lightly toasted, no cream cheese, that one wants butter, and the other one wants his bagel half with jelly, half plain...) It's enough to make anyone lose it. But if you take a moment to realize you are fulfilling the mitzvah of emulating God, it's likely to bring a smile to your face, at least for a few seconds!

Another way to act like God is to be a creator. Now that doesn't mean you have to be creative by nature. It means creating opportunities to find and share meaning with your kids, your friends, or your spouse. Bake a birthday cake with your child instead of picking one up at the bakery and watch what happens. Your personal investment creates excitement and appreciation.

> *"My son likes to help in the kitchen. He wanted to make a birthday cake for his brother. So I took him to the store, let him pick a fun-shaped cake pan, frosting, decorating ices, and a mix. He picked an ambitious racecar mold. Sure enough the cake didn't rise fully and came out of the pan with more than one flat tire. This brought tears and anger. So much for being a creator! But then I had the idea to make some brownie cupcakes and turn them into chocolatey wheels. It ended up even better than we thought!" Leah*

There is a passage in the Torah (Exodus 34:6-7) that describes the attributes of God: "Merciful God, powerful God, compassionate and gracious, slow to anger, and abundant in kindness and truth. Preserver of kindness for thousands of generations, forgiver of iniquity, willful sin and error..." The Talmud comments: "Just as He is merciful, you should be merciful, just as He is compassionate, you should be compassionate, just as He is holy, you should be holy." It's helpful to keep these ideas in mind as we interact with our children, friends and yes, even mothers-in-law. Taking the proverbial high road usually leads to someplace good.

There is a concept in Judaism known as *derech eretz* which literally means the way of the land. It is more commonly understood as being a good person with good character. Our sages say that being a considerate, kind and respectful person actually comes before learning Torah. Being a mensch is a mitzvah.

GOD IS ONE

It is safe to say that if you are a Jew regardless of background and practice, you have heard of the *Shema:* the quintessential statement of monotheism meaning: "Hear, O Israel, the Lord our God, the Lord is one."

This statement embodies the important commandment to know that God is one. What does this really mean? And how can we fulfill this mitzvah? Within every living being, there is a spark of holiness. Every person and animal contains a small piece of the Creator. So does every tree and flower and mountain. Since we know there is only one God, we are by extension, part of that oneness.

5

GOD IS ONE

The clear blue sky, the broken air conditioner, the dinner you have to shop for and cook, the soccer practice, the eye doctor appointment, the hug that envelopes you in puppy-dog sweetness, the book you can't put down, the strong, hot cup of Earl Grey tea with honey ... it's all one continuous gift from God!

This oneness also extends to every human being with whom you come in contact with. From the mailman to the bus driver to the teacher who has it out for your son. Remembering that we are all in this together helps keep you connected to each other and to God. The numerical value for the Hebrew word one *(echod)* equals the same numerical value for the Hebrew word love *(ahava)*.

ALL YOU NEED IS LOVE

"And you shall love the Lord, your God, with all your heart and with all your soul and with all your resources." Deuteronomy 6:5

The second paragraph of the *Shema* commands us to love God. Rabbi Akiva, the great second century sage, said you could sum up the whole Torah in one word: "love."

Cultivating a personal, loving relationship with God may not come naturally to some. It's hard to hang out with someone you can't see or hear. Let alone have a conversation with the supernal Provider. "I mean, how can little old me even consider connecting with the Creator?!" This concept is completely foreign to many.

"I don't believe there's a God that pays attention to our everyday lives. My life is far too small to be of importance to anyone but me and my immediate family." Rachel

But, of course God in His infinite wisdom and generosity gives each of us countless ways to make that connection every single day. Whether it's saying a blessing before chowing down that bran muffin or kissing the front door mezuzah after putting 47 more miles on the minivan, the mitzvahs that God gives us are the roadmap to a lifetime of love. And though it might feel strange to do some of these rituals at first, especially if we were not raised this way, glimpses and rushes of love will break through.

"I talk to God all day. I tell him my problems, what I want to accomplish, how I'm feeling...that I really need to find a parking spot. It makes the relationship more tangible—even if I do get some strange looks..." Shelly

HAVE SOME FEAR

"To fear Him reverently." Deuteronomy 6:13; 10:20

As important as it is to cultivate a love of God, fear of God is a fundamental commandment as well. How can fearing God be a mitzvah as applied to everyday life? Fearing God does not mean worrying that a bolt of lightning will shoot down from the sky if you do something wrong.

The Hebrew word *yirah* is more accurately translated as "awe." It also shares the root "to see." This can be experienced when you look in your child's eyes or see a star-filled sky or stand on the rim of the Grand Canyon. The "fear" if you will, of God is a constant awareness of His divine presence and guidance in your everyday life. And knowing that what you do day to day with the precious gifts He's given you has real meaning and consequences.

When used positively, fear is the ultimate motivator. Fearing God can help you spend your time and energy wisely and consciously. Everyone wants purpose and meaning in their lives. Fear can keep you on track. Instead of surfing the web to buy more things you don't even need, you might surf the web for interesting Torah articles or classes instead (okay, I admit both are guilty pleasures for me!).

> *"I couldn't wait until my kids went off to summer camp. No cooking, no cleaning, no laundry. Just shopping, and movies and restaurants and traveling...But as soon as they left, I found myself doing other things; like visiting a sick friend and not running out after 20 minutes, catching up on all the graduation and baby gifts, making phone calls to people I hadn't spoken with.... The summer weeks without my kids were a gift, but so not the one I expected." Eva*

WON'T YOU PLEASE LOVE YOUR NEIGHBOR?

"Love your neighbor as yourself." Leviticus 19:18

This mitzvah is widely known by Jews and non-Jews alike. There is also the partner commandment "Do not hate your brother." (Leviticus 19:17). The fact that the same mitzvah is written two different ways underscores its inherent importance. But how do you do that? How do you actually love people who are not family or intimate friends?

The first step to loving others is to love yourself. Pop psychology labeled it "I'm Ok, you're Ok." Since reams have been written on the subject you don't have to take my laywoman's word for it, but self love is the only way to be able to love others. If you need a pep talk for self love just think about the fact that God in all his infinite wisdom and power chose to create only one "YOU" for all eternity. Can you feel the love?

The Jewish people and the world at large are more closely connected than you might first think. Each of us has a holy piece of God within us and all these sparks are part of one entity (remember God is One). There is a famous tale of a Rabbi from Jerusalem named Aryeh Levin who goes to the doctor with his wife and says "Our leg hurts." By realizing the deep human connection that exists, love is the natural response. The notion of *ahavas yisroel* or love of the entire Jewish people is a central theme of the Chassidic movement. When a Jew 5000 miles away suffers, we feel his or her pain and want to help. We all know this firsthand by sharing both the suffering and the ultimate joy of Gilad Shalit. It is a commandment to help fellow Jews everywhere in the world because as discussed earlier, we are all one. Just as baseless hatred was the cause of the destruction of the holy Temple, Jews believe that ultimately the Messiah will come through the mitzvah of loving your fellow Jew.

So the next time you give your neighbor a ride to the auto shop, or watch your friend's kids or drop off a meal for someone sitting shiva, you are doing more than just being nice.

LOVE YOUR NEIGHBOR EVEN IF YOU DON'T LOVE WHAT THEY'RE DOING

"You shall judge your fellow with righteousness." Vayikra 19:15

Another aspect of loving your neighbor is judging him or her favorably. Basically it's giving everyone the benefit of the doubt. What does this mean on a practical level? Not jumping to conclusions because of something you see or hear. Taking a moment to get outside your own head and step into someone else's shoes. A huge part of judging people favorably is not taking things personally. So if you didn't react to someone's tone on the phone or glaring look at the store, you just did a mitzvah!!

LOVE YOUR NEIGHBOR EVEN IF YOU DON'T LOVE WHAT THEY'RE DOING

"I was waiting for my friend on a street corner in the rain. She was five minutes late, then 10, then 15. I tried to remain calm, telling myself she must have some reason for not being there. Finally, I stepped under an awning to call her cell phone. She cheerfully picked the phone. I told her I was waiting and she told me we were supposed have lunch next Wednesday!" Miriam

A little empathy can go a long way. This means keeping your cool when someone cuts you off in traffic. It means picking up your neighbor's garbage can lids that blew into your yard. It means smiling at salespeople even if you've had a stressful morning.

There's a Kabalistic idea that the type and amount of energy you put out into the universe will come back to you. That is also what the bestselling book, *The Secret* by Rhonda Byrne, maintains. The most amazing part is that it actually works! See what happens when you go through your day grumpy. Watch the energy in your house deflate when you are in a lousy mood. Even if you don't feel great, acting happy will do the trick! Sometimes you have to "fake it to make it!"

{ 10 }

MORE LOVE

"Love the stranger." Deuteronomy 10:19

It's not just yourself and your neighbor and your fellow Jew God commands you to love, you must also love the stranger. Who is the stranger? Anyone who is not comfortable in their surroundings. Historically Jews were strangers in a strange land. God wants us to use our own sensitivity to discomfort to help others feel more at ease.

The commandment to love God, yourself, your neighbor, your fellow Jew, the stranger and of course Torah itself is synonymous with being a Jew. Just like guarding our health (bodies) allows us to physically perform the other mitzvahs, the commandment to love allows us to spiritually connect to our Creator and the world in the most meaningful way possible.

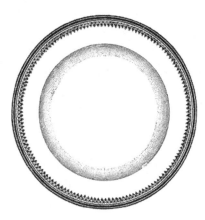

OPEN HOUSE

The Jewish notion of hospitality is as old as the Torah. Fortunately, we all inherit a strong trait of welcoming guests from our patriarchs and matriarchs. In the book of Genesis, Abraham's tent was open on all sides. Sarah never balked at an extra 150 unexpected Shabbos guests. Abraham even tended to passersby *before* he responded to God himself! Abraham's generosity was not limited to meeting his guests' basic needs. He and his wife went above and beyond to shower visitors with abundance and variety.

When you open your home to friends and strangers alike, you are doing a mitzvah. This resonates with me because I am no Martha Stewart. I get stressed when one couple comes over for one meal.

11

OPEN HOUSE

Imagine my anxiety when my husband told me he invited a family of 11 to stay with us for Shabbat. An Orthodox Rabbi and his nine kids!! Plus my family of five times four meals is 64 plates, knifes and forks!! I was a basket-case leading up to the weekend. Gradually as Friday night ended, I became more comfortable and by the end of Shabbos, was filled with such a sense of satisfaction and accomplishment, I thought I could actually do it all over again! (And yes, I actually did!)

Getting outside my own comfort zone and opening my home for meals, community events, and classes has opened my eyes and heart in ways I never would have expected. The fact that a Jew can find a warm and welcoming home almost anywhere in the world is an amazing reality.

Welcoming guests is not limited to your home. My rabbi told me the following story:

> *"I was in a tiny coffee shop in Brooklyn with only three little tables. I settled in one of the chairs with my stack of papers and coffee when an elderly man came in and was looking for a place to sit. I cleared off an area at my table, pulled out a chair and offered him a newspaper to read. You don't have to be in your home to welcome guests!"* > *Rabbi B*

HOLD YOUR TONGUE

"Do not wrong anyone in speech." Leviticus 25:17

The commandment not to speak derogatorily of others is one of the most written about mitzvahs of all. There are hundreds of books on the subject, also known as *lashon hara*. The Chofetz Chaim dedicated his life to delineating the conditions of proper and improper speech. He put it succinctly: "One who speaks *lashon hara* attaches himself to a practice that destroys the world."

Why? Because speaking or listening to bad speech goes against our purpose in life. We all know juicy gossip is alluring, infectious and thrilling. But we also know words can inflict irreversible damage, often greater than physical abuse. We see firsthand the tragic results of cyber-bullying. Words can destroy, just as words can create. According to the Torah's opening passages, God created the world with words. He said, "Let there be light!" And there was light. The ability to form words and speak is the thing that separates man from animal.

Awareness of words is a good first step. The next time you're out for lunch or in a social situation, make a mental note of the quality of the conversation. More often than not it will deteriorate into some sort of gossip. There is actually a commandment not to carry tales (Leviticus 19:16). You can do this mitzvah by not initiating gossip and by not taking the bait. A great technique is changing the subject. If someone is cornering you, digging for dirt, just say you're uncomfortable and move on.

Another step towards proper speech is setting aside an hour or two every day when you promise yourself you will not, under any circumstances, speak *lashon hara*. You can do this with a group of friends dividing the day into different time slots. If two hours seems overwhelming, start with 15 minutes.

> *"A terminally ill father at my sons' Jewish day school asked all the children to not speak lashon hara for the short time he had left. His dying wish made a lasting impression on the whole community."*
> *Gail*

The Torah specifically forbids cursing your fellow Jew (Leviticus 14:19). Disharmony among Jews is a historical fact with tragic consequences. With differing practices and philosophies, bad-mouthing your fellow Jew seems like your God-given right. Just remember it's completely the opposite.

Not speaking *lashon hara* also applies to yourself. That means you cannot put yourself down!! Whether berating yourself internally or criticizing yourself among friends, this behavior is simply not allowed. So the next time you catch yourself "beating yourself up" over who knows what, be aware of what you're doing and go back to the commandment of "love your neighbor as yourself."

By restricting our behavior, we elevate our souls and make connecting to God possible. To an outsider, such restrictions can appear to be limitations. And if they didn't come from God who runs the world, they actually would be. But just like you know what's best for your child, God knows what's best for us. So He tells us: "Think before you speak." Or like my mom always said to me, "If you don't have something nice to say, don't say anything at all." Or was that from Bambi?

KEEPING YOUR WORD

"Do not violate an oath or swear falsely." Leviticus 19:12

The Torah commands us not to make promises we can't keep. Even with the best intentions, the outcome of what we vow is out of our control. There is a Hebrew expression *bli neder* which means "without commitment" that many observant people add to the end of "promises." For example, "I'll take your kids to the Bronx Zoo sometime this summer, bli neder." This qualifies the commitment by absolving the speaker from not keeping her word.

If you do find yourself in a situation where a vow or oath seems necessary, choose your words carefully. A subtle shift from "I prom-

KEEPING YOUR WORD

ise or I swear…" to "I hope I can….or I plan on….." can make a big difference in keeping your word. It also gives you credibility and builds trust. This is especially helpful in relationships with family. It avoids the classic retort "but you promised!!"

NAME DROPPING

"Hallow God's name." Leviticus 22:32

There are three separate commandments regarding the name of God. One positive: *to revere his name* and *two negative: not to blaspheme or take His name in vain.* When we say God's name in anything other than prayer or reverence or gratitude, we are doing the opposite of a mitzvah. We are slinging the greatest insult without as much as a second thought.

Being raised in a secular world, saying "Oh God," to just about anything is fairly commonplace. OMG is right up there with LOL. Or worse, stringing it together with some other expletives can be a knee jerk reaction. I've even caught myself doing this to no one in particular....in my car during traffic or stubbing my toe in the dark.

By catching yourself and stopping or substituting "gosh" if you need to, you're actually doing a mitzvah. This can extend to all cursing for that matter. Remember it's the mouth that connects you directly to God. And the example you set for family and friends can speak volumes.

> *"We have a swear jar in our house. The kids made a list of offensive words with the corresponding fines. Unfortunately the jar does get filled, but then we decide together which charity will benefit from our mistakes!" Jill*

HOW EMBARRASSING

"Do not put any Jew to shame." Leviticus 19:17

Directly related to improper speech, is the mitzvah of not embarrassing others. This may be my own Achilles' heel as I am quick with the clever barb to elicit the laugh. I am ashamed to admit how many times I have embarrassed my husband and, gulp, even my kids.

If you have to follow up a comment with "I was only joking," then, chances are, you hit a nerve. Being funny at no one's expense is far more difficult than taking pot shots. It's an entirely different level of humor that can make people smile for the right reasons.

15

HOW EMBARRASSING

Embarrassing others and speaking lashon hara can also be non-verbal. Often times, much can be said with a look, a turn of the back or a roll of the eyes. You can undo someone with a simple gesture. Be aware of your body language and the vibe you are putting out there. A simple wave of the hand, nod of the head or smile can mean more mitzvahs in the world.

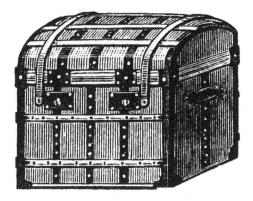

GIVE UP THE GRUDGE

"Do not bear a grudge." Leviticus 19:18

I was surprised to find out that not bearing a grudge was actually a mitzvah written in the Torah. Why would God care if you had a bone to pick with someone? Because God wants us to love each other (remember all those love commandments?!). It's far more difficult to love someone when you're holding on to a big heavy dose of resentment.

Do you ever run into someone and have a negative reaction from the past? "Oh, there's so and so, she never calls me back." Or, "Did you see how she stood there and ignored me?!" Or, is there a person you avoid at the supermarket, hoping she won't notice you squirming down the aisle? Grudge alert!!

Forgiveness is a fundamental part of Judaism. We pray for it collectively and individually every Yom Kippur. It is also a part of daily and nightly prayers. Jewish law (known as *halacha*) dictates that we must ask forgiveness directly of those we have wronged. Conversely, we have an obligation to grant forgiveness to those who ask it of us if we are the injured party.

In addition, the virtue of peace is the most cherished value of Judaism. Whatever it takes, whatever the cost, peace is the goal.

"I hadn't spoken with my sister in close to three years. She had done something to me that I felt was unforgiveable. It took my father having a stroke to bring us back into the same room. When I saw her the anger melted immediately and what she had done didn't matter at all. Why had I waited so long to realize this?" Ellen

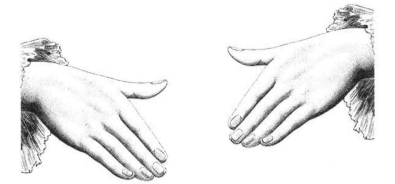

REVENGE IS NOT SO SWEET

"Do not take revenge." Leviticus 19:18

If you can successfully not bear a grudge, then the need for revenge disappears. Unfortunately for most of us mortals, seeking revenge can be cathartic. "I'm not inviting her because she dissed me! That'll show her!"

Movies and books romanticize the notion of revenge. There are even websites dedicated to getting even. The word "frenemy" is now officially recognized in the dictionary!

Taking revenge only perpetuates a conflict. The Torah perspective is to either judge someone favorably (as mentioned earlier) or to

REVENGE IS NOT SO SWEET

confront the person to give them a chance to explain or apologize. Revenge might feel good in the moment, but the damage lasts forever. Resisting the urge to get back at someone is a mitzvah everyone can benefit from.

{ 18 }

STUMBLING BLOCK

"Do not curse a deaf person or place a stumbling block before the blind."
Leviticus 19:14

How often do we find ourselves cursing the deaf and tripping the blind? Surprisingly, more often than you might realize. This commandment, simply put, suggests never play to someone's weakness.

If your friend is on a strict diet, you should not be serving tempting desserts. If your mom gets upset when you talk about your Uncle Morty, don't talk about your Uncle Morty! You shouldn't be talking about Uncle Morty anyway if you're not speaking *lashon hara!*

This is a subtle mitzvah because we don't always take the time to

18

STUMBLING BLOCK

examine people's weaknesses or triggers. It brings us back to the commandment to love your neighbor. If we're empathetic and sensitive, we take the time to consider things from someone else's view. We don't want to set someone up for failure.

This relates to children too. You should not expect your child to be musical or artistic or outgoing just because you are. The Talmud says, "Raise each child up according to his ways." It doesn't say over-program your child so they'll have a good resume. Nurture the strengths that God blessed your child with and watch what happens. Taking piano lessons can be a mitzvah for one child and stopping them can be a mitzvah for another.

HOME SWEET HOME

There is a concept in Judaism known as *shalom bayit* which translates as "peace in the home." It is a mitzvah that often supersedes other mitzvahs. Peace in the home should be a constant priority at all costs.

Just as volumes have been written on *lashon hara,* there are many books dedicated to *shalom bayit.* This mitzvah incorporates many others that have already been mentioned, like holding your tongue, not bearing a grudge and granting forgiveness.

Judaism holds marriage between husband and wife to be the ultimate relationship. More important than parent to child, child to parent or sibling to sibling. This means that when a husband puts his dirty briefcase (that's been on the floor of every public train, bus and bathroom) on the kitchen table, the wife can't scream at him! (Well she *can*, but she *shouldn't!*) She has to take a few cleansing breaths and suggest a better place for it. This also means that when the husband gives the kids ice cream for breakfast, the wife has to focus on the fact that he actually gave them breakfast, praise him and then privately offer up some healthier alternatives.

This obviously holds for both sides of the equation. The husband has to politely listen to the wife download her day without looking at his Blackberry. He should set an example for the kids, clean up after himself, thank his wife for the delicious dinner and help his children with their homework!!

Everyday we have the chance to do the mitzvah of *shalom bayit*. And very often the best technique is not to do or say anything. Silence is a very powerful tool. Our sages say there is nothing better for us physically and spiritually than silence. That means not reacting, not disrespecting, not judging. Peace can be more easily achieved if we are not trying to be right, make our point, or control others. There is no precise formula for *shalom bayit* because every marriage is a unique joining of souls with unique needs. But on some gut level we all intuit when we are moving towards peace or rocking the boat.

Anyone who has been in a home that lacks *shalom bayit* can actually feel a palpable vibe of discomfort and disharmony. If you can feel the tension, imagine what it is doing to the innocent children who live with it everyday. Promoting *shalom bayit,* like guarding your health, provides the right environment to achieve the many commandments God has given us.

AMERICAN IDOLS

"Do not make a graven image; neither to make it oneself nor to have it made by others." Exodus 20:4

"Do not minister to an idol. Do not worship an idol." Exodus 20:5

Idolatry is mentioned repeatedly in the Torah with many commandments forbidding the making and worshipping of idols and even talking about them. And the commandment not to make graven images is right up there in the big ten.

Terach, who was Abraham's father, was an idol worshipper. So was Laban, Rachel and Leah's father. As is the case with everything mentioned in the Torah, no detail is insignificant. Egypt epitomized idolatry and materialism. Many Jews could not break free from the allure even when they were given the chance to leave.

Perhaps the most famous example of idolatry in the Torah is the golden calf. When Moses didn't return promptly, impatience and desperation took over. And the golden calf was the result. One important fact: women did not participate in the building of the golden calf. This is a great reminder and indication of the women's innate connection to the spiritual. That connection can easily get lost or shaky, but it is there.

Jews today obviously do not bow down to graven images, but we are all idol worshippers of some sort. We worship money. We crave power. We glorify celebrity. We idealize being thin. We are slaves to our anger. Judaism holds that any belief, practice or action which interferes with our relationship with God can be considered idol worship.

These "idols" can be very tempting, but they are distractions and impediments to real spiritual growth. Who hasn't fallen into the "if only" trap? "If only I were 10 pounds lighter, if only I had a bigger kitchen, if only I got that job ... if only I could write this book!"

"My mom tells of her friend Joan who was the first in her community to redo her kitchen. Granite countertops, hand-painted backsplash, ceramic tile floor, all state-of-the-art appliances. It was a shrine of sorts and she kept it immaculate, never cluttering the counters with any signs of life, rarely cooking a meal lest she get her Wolf cooktop-dirty! My mother also recounts that at this same woman's shiva,

AMERICAN IDOLS

these same counters were so plastered with platters and kugels and flowers and cards, you could hardly see the granite." Leah

This doesn't mean you can't enjoy material things. You do not have to live in a cave like Rabbi Shimon bar Yochai! But using fine things as means of connecting with God is the ultimate goal. Acquiring more things as an end in itself is the danger to avoid.

Shopping is often very therapeutic, exhilarating and relaxing at the same time. I admit I have reached a zen state at Century 21 (a discount store in New York), losing all sense of time and reason. I manage to elevate the experience by buying just the right gift for someone else, clothes for my kids or getting a special hat for the High Holidays ... reminding myself of the bigger picture while soaking up the satisfaction of a good bargain. You can turn shopping from a mindless distraction to a purposeful mitzvah. It's all in the way you frame it.

ENVY OF ALL

"Do not to covet what belongs to another." Exodus 20:14

"Do not desire another's possessions." Deuteronomy 5:18

There are two mitzvahs in the Torah related to jealousy. The notion that the grass is always greener seems second nature. Who doesn't look over their shoulder and think: "She has a better figure, drives a nicer car, has a bigger house, bakes a sweeter challah,"…the list is endless.

Why do we find ourselves in these constant bouts of comparison? The answer is two-fold. One is that the *yatzer harah* (the negative

ENVY OF ALL

inclination) is very strong and battles for our attention all the time. Your ego will tell you, "You deserve better, you should have what you want." Someone once gave the acronym for ego as Edging God Out. This sense of entitlement is exactly that. The second part of the equation is that we aren't truly grateful for what we do have. God gives each of us our unique set of strengths, challenges, blessings and hardships. Though it is sometimes hard to believe this, He gives us exactly what is perfect for each and every one of us.

Rather than feeling covetous, envious, or bitter, try seeing others' success as something perfect for them. Be happy your neighbor could afford a new kitchen. Rejoice that your niece got engaged (even if your own daughter is having trouble finding a husband). What other people have has absolutely nothing to do with your happiness. Faith and trust in the Almighty has everything to do with it. To quote Esther Bayla Schwarz, "Life is not a competition!" So the next time you catch yourself eyeing your friend's necklace longingly—compliment her instead. And see how good it makes both of you feel.

YOU LEARN SOMETHING NEW EVERYDAY

"Learn Torah and…teach it." Deuteronomy 6:7

There are several commandments in the Torah about studying Torah. You should not only learn and teach Torah, you should respect those who know Torah and teach it. My husband has a habit of kissing every rabbi he meets (this can seriously freak out some rabbis). He says "I kiss the Torah. And rabbis are the embodiment of Torah, so I kiss them too!"

Okay, so we are supposed to learn Torah! It's a big mitzvah, but the very idea can seem intimidating, overwhelming not to mention vague. How do we go about it? Just crack the Five Books open and start reading?

LEARN SOMETHING NEW EVERYDAY

First, decide what you want to learn about. There are potentially countless aspects of Torah study with equally endless commentaries. A popular choice is the Torah portion (*parsha*) of the week. You can do this in a structured weekly class, or on your own by reading books or going online and reading commentaries on various websites. (My favorites are included at the end of this book.) Some classes concentrate on decoding and dissecting the text; others extrapolate lessons from the verses and apply them to modern times and everyday lives. Find a class that interests you. The most incredible thing about studying the Torah portion is the never ending supply of information and insight that comes out of what seems like just a story. The fact that you can look at the same words and get new meaning every time makes learning an ongoing journey. Even the wisest, most learned scholars keep finding new layers of understanding their entire lives.

Another way of tackling Torah study is to find a teacher who inspires you. A mentor is crucial for sustained spiritual growth. There are endless gifted writers and speakers, men and women, out there. You just have to make the effort to find them. And with the internet, you can e-mail many of these people directly and get almost instantaneous feedback. As I researched this book, I found the web invaluable in providing all kinds of answers to almost any question I could think of (Googling with God).

What about the kids? All parents are commanded to teach their children Torah. The beauty of this is that many times you can learn along with your kids. Every Shabbat we print out a family *parsha* story from www.aish.com. My husband asks one of our boys to read it out loud, and then we all answer the follow up questions. It always makes for interesting conversation and sparks further questions.

You can also turn the tables and ask your children to teach you something about the weekly *parsha*. Have them prepare something in advance in any form they want (drawings, poems, puzzles) and share it with the family. This mitzvah also enriches the mitzvah of keeping Shabbat.

Furthermore, keep in mind that by doing all the mitzvahs in this book and doing them with joy, you are teaching your children Torah. Every time you light Shabbat candles, kiss the mezuzah, treat your spouse or parents with respect, don't scream even though the kids are fighting and the chicken is burning, you are transmitting Torah values.

Sometimes when tragedy strikes and you feel powerless. Learning something new from the Torah or adding a mitzvah to your repertoire can feel pro-active and bring comfort. When a good friend of ours was diagnosed with colon cancer, I decided to learn *Asher Yatzar* (the prayer said after using the bathroom) in the merit of his recovery. I photocopied it and stuck it on the wall so I could learn it. (One year later, I am happy to report he is fully recovered and I have one more Hebrew prayer memorized!)

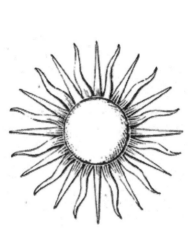

A PRAYER OR TWO EACH DAY

"Pray to God." Deuteronomy 6:13 (Note the chapter and verse numbers!)

"Say the Shema in the morning and at night." Deuteronomy 6:7

Prayer is central to Judaism. It is considered one of the three pillars (along with good deeds and tzedakah). Like much of Jewish tradition, prayer can be overwhelming, intimidating and difficult, even if you *have* been raised observant. Rest assured it is not quantity of prayers, but quality and connection during praying.

The first prayer commandment is often worded as "serve" God. This can take the pressure off of the technical aspect of knowing which prayers to say and when to say them. Instead, ask yourself is what I'm doing, where I'm going, whom I'm seeing serving God? If you want to take on a more concrete approach with specific prayers, start small. I know from personal experience that being overly ambitious makes the learning curve even steeper. For starters say *Modeh Ani* in the morning in English or Hebrew. You should say it the moment your feet touch the ground. Once you master that, you can say the blessing over washing your hands. After that you can open a siddur and recite the morning blessings. It helps to have someone knowledgeable walk you through the prayer book. There are audio files online that you can download to help you read and pronounce the Hebrew words. I find having a tune to be helpful with absorbing new prayer. You can even make up your own or put the words to a melody you like. Just remember, small mindful steps.

Saying the *Shema* is another great way to bookend your day. Once in the morning and once at night is a comforting reminder of God's constant presence in your life. This is also a meaningful ritual to share with your children before they go to bed. It is something they can do on their own that can give them great comfort.

While there is great wisdom, insight and order to formalized prayer, you can pray spontaneously and in your own words. You can praise, thank and ask God for things all day long. It is best to actually vocalize your prayers at a low audible level (as opposed to thinking them in your head). Saying them out loud makes them concrete and helps you clarify your priorities. It also helps solidify your connection to God.

"Preparing for Passover kept me so busy, I didn't really have time to pray. So with each closet I cleaned and brisket I roasted, I said a special prayer out loud for each member of my family. It made the preparation less of a chore and more of a blessing." Esther

Writing down your own personal prayer is another option. I keep mine in my computer and update it as needed.

AGE OLD SECRET

"Honor the old and the wise." Leviticus 19:32

The Torah commands us to respect our elders. Not so easy in a society where old age is not revered. If anything, aging is the enemy. How many millions of dollars are spent every year in a desperate attempt to hold on to youth?

The Torah sees growing old as a positive. The Hebrew word for elderly is *zaken* which is an acronym for *"zeh shekaneh chachma"* – a person who has acquired wisdom. The Talmud states that the respect we owe the elderly applies to Torah scholars and non-Torah scholars, Jews and non-Jews (Kidushin 32b).

24

AGE OLD SECRET

Since we value the physical (often more than the spiritual), youth and strength are vital commodities. But Judaism holds that the older you get, the less you rely on the physical body and the more you become a soul. Being more of a soul and less of a body is what we strive for everyday and the elderly inherently have it!

This gives new meaning to "respect your elders." By taking the time to appreciate the holiness of an older person, you are performing a mitzvah. It's not just the proverbial helping the old lady across the street. It's much deeper than that. It's an ideological shift that can enrich your relationships and your life.

DEAR MOM AND DAD

"Honor your father and your mother." Exodus 20:12, Deuteronomy 5:16

"Fear your mother and your father." Leviticus 19:3

"Do not to curse your father or mother." Exodus 21:17

There are three commandments in the Torah pertaining to parents. Honoring them. fearing them and not cursing them. The commandments are written in such a way that doing so for *both* a mother *and* a father are equal. There are obvious parental parallels between God and His children (us) and parents (us) and our children. This commandment appears as number five of the original ten, occupying the middle place between commandments between man and God and commandments between man and man. To say it is the most challenging, complex relationship we experience in life may be the reason the Talmud declares honoring one's parents to be the most difficult commandment to follow properly.

The Talmud states that honoring ones parents can be fulfilled by providing for their physical needs; such as food and shelter. Cursing or embarrassing your mother or father or even mother-in-law or father-in-law is tantamount to blaspheming God. Just as God created man, your parents with God's help created you. This commandment holds even after a parent has passed away.

Fearing your mother and father is similar to the "awe" commandment to fear God. An example from the Talmud is not to sit in your father or mother's chair and not to contradict what a parent says. Respect for ones parents is a mandate for self-respect.

Interestingly enough it is not a commandment to *love* your mother and father. The unconditional love is reserved for God only. God knows that love flows from parent to child and not necessarily in the opposite direction. This is another affirmation of God's love for each and every one of us.

So what about very difficult parents? A mother who constantly criticizes? Or a father who is cold and unfeeling? Must we honor them? The answer is yes. It is more about the behavior than the feeling. And while it is often easier to see your mother and father's faults, there are bound to be positive attributes you can focus on as

DEAR MOM AND DAD

well. Their combination of character traits, both good and bad, are the basis of who we are today.

> *"I've had a strained relationship with my mother my whole adult life. Nothing I did was ever good enough. Every family gathering ended up in a battle. I felt sad that we couldn't get along because she seemed fine with my brothers and sister. Then I decided I wouldn't say anything negative to her or about her. This was no easy task. At first I felt like I would explode. But over time things did improve. And while it's still not ideal, I found using this tool to be very helpful."* Beth

The Torah says that honoring your mother and father can extend your life on earth in case you need further motivation! On a very practical level, fulfilling this mitzvah can be as simple as sending a photo or email or note, picking up the phone or holding your tongue (hopefully not in that order!).

TGIF (NIGHT)

"Sanctify Shabbat." Exodus 20:8

"Do not work on Shabbat." Exodus 20:10

"Rest on Shabbat." Exodus 23:12; 34:21

Of all the mitzvahs in this book, observing Shabbat is my personal favorite. Brilliant in its conception and ever more relevant in today's age of technology, Shabbat is 25 hours of old fashioned quality time. No phone to answer, no emails to send, no errands to run, no mind-numbing TV or computer…it's the ultimate chance to unplug from the fast-paced world and plug into the spiritual.

"I could never keep Shabbos! It's way too hard. I mean what do you do all day?!" Tracy

Observing all the laws and commandments can be overwhelming, intimidating and confusing. Many people view Shabbat as a time of don't and can't. Understanding the reasons for the restrictions can help shift your perspective. Like most things in Judaism, small steps make all the difference. Some people start with Friday night dinner.

"I started by not going out Friday nights. I would rent a movie and stay home. Then I started choosing movies with Jewish themes. Then I stopped watching movies and started having people over for a meal and conversation. Gradually over the next ten years as I learned more, I added hours and rituals. Now my husband and six children joyfully celebrate Shabbos every week. I don't know what life would be like without it." Chana

Shabbat is a day to recognize that God is the supreme Creator. If we never take the time to stop creating ourselves, it is easy to think that we make things happen! Only by stopping our hectic, non-stop daily routines, can we take the time to fully grasp God's limitless power and wonder.

The sages say that we all receive an extra soul on Shabbat. That during the week one soul is enough, but Shabbat is so holy and spiritual, we need two souls to fully appreciate it. Use your double dose of soul to connect with God and family and friends in a way you can't during the rest of week.

CHALLAH DAY

One of the special mitzvahs associated with Shabbat is the making and taking and baking of Challah. The mixing of flour (physical) and water (Torah) is another way God gave us to elevate the ordinary.

The technical aspect of following this commandment involves taking a small piece of dough (made with a specific amount of flour) after it is kneaded but before it is baked and setting it aside. This represents an offering to God from the days of the Holy Temple. Since we have no Temple today, we burn or discard this Challah after separating it and saying a blessing. Women speak of a special connection at this moment when they speak directly to God and say personal prayers.

CHALLAH DAY

"I find the kneading to be very therapeutic. I really lose myself in the repetitive motion. And I can also get some of my frustrations from the week out!" Nancy

"The smell alone is reason enough to make Challah. The house is filled with this heavenly scent!" Mimi

"When I pull out the golden loaves that have magically transformed, I feel the miracle of Shabbat." Susan

It seems that like many of the mitzvahs in this book, making Challah is a process. Do not get discouraged if your first try is burnt or raw or heavy as a brick. Like most meaningful things in life, it's trial and error. An extra dollop of honey, one less egg, a dash of cinnamon, the right bowl…God knows you will find your way.

THE LIGHT OF SHABBAT

It is a mitzvah to usher in Shabbat by lighting candles. It is customary to give tzedakah before performing this ritual to enrich one mitzvah with another. Lighting takes place 18 minutes before sunset. Women cover their heads, light the candles, move their hands over the candles, cover their eyes and recite the blessing. This is the technical explanation of the mitzvah. But what does it all mean?

On a literal level, you are bringing light into the home. Light is an extension of God. As it says in the Torah, God created light and it was good. So you too are creating a place of holiness and goodness.

29

THE LIGHT OF SHABBAT

On a deeper level, lighting the Shabbat candles is a spiritual connection with our Creator. Many women take a moment after lighting to pray for their family's well being. Just like we light candles for a romantic dinner, lighting the Shabbat candles symbolizes our deep love for and gratitude to God.

Even in the midst of the pre-Shabbat scramble, kids screaming in the background, doors slamming; take a moment or two for your soul to absorb the peace of the mitzvah of candlelighting.

THE OBVIOUS MITZVAHS

Giving charity, feeding the hungry, clothing the naked, visiting the sick….these are the quintessential "good deed" mitzvahs; the "Miss America" mitzvahs fighting poverty, illness and misfortune.

Because they are universal and global, they often seem vague and lofty. How can I fight world hunger? The Jewish community makes these mitzvahs tangible. The place to start is your neighborhood or town or city. There are programs through synagogues to visit the sick. Unfortunately everyone has people in their lives who aren't well. You don't have to visit a stranger. There are Tomchei Shabbos programs giving food to people who need. There are tzedakah boxes in local stores. There are clothing drives and drop off containers.

THE OBVIOUS MITZVAHS

Involve your children in these mitzvahs by cleaning out their closets and toy chests with them. Take them to a soup kitchen or food warehouse and let them serve meals or pack boxes. These experiences are eternal gifts.

It says in the Torah that you are supposed to give charity according to your means (Deuteronomy 15:11). This often translates to 10% of your income (tithing) and up to 20% of your profits. There's a philosophy that the money you have at your disposal is not really "yours." God made it possible for you to have it in order to use it wisely. The ideal way to give tzedakah is anonymously, no big plaque on the building, no photo in the paper. If you need the accolades, don't let that stop you from giving generously.

In terms of priorities of giving, family comes first. If a cousin in Cleveland needs financial help, that supersedes the orphanage in Israel. Similarly local community comes before global foundations. This helps give structure to giving and assures each ripple in the pond of need gets its due.

{ 3 1 }

EVERGREEN

Long before recycling and environmental protection, the Torah commanded us to take care of the planet. One of the first commandments is for man "to work and tend the land." (Genesis 2:15) There is a midrash that says God showed Adam all the trees in the Garden of Eden and said "all I created, I created for you. Beware lest you spoil and destroy my world, for if you will spoil it, there is no one to repair it after you."(Ecclesiastes Rabbah 7:13)

There is a law called *bal tashchit*, which prohibits the destruction of fruit trees during war (Deuteronomy 20:19). Over the years, its rabbinical interpretation has broadened to forbidding any needless destruction or waste to nature. There are also several commandments to observe the sabbatical year, when the land must rest every seven years.

The Torah predates the growing "green" trend by thousands of years. So the next time you take your own bags to the grocery store, plant your own garden, clean up trash around your neighborhood or drive a hybrid car, you are being more than environmentally conscious. You are fulfilling God's commandments to protect and preserve this beautiful world.

WOW! NEVER KNEW THAT WAS A MITZVAH!

Here are some self-explanatory practical common sense mitzvahs straight from the Torah: Pay wages on time (Leviticus 19:13). So pay the handyman now instead of later! Return a lost object (Deuteronomy 22:1), no finders-keepers here. Be compassionate to animals (Deuteronomy 22:6) the predecessor to PETA! There is actually a commandment to feed your animals *before* you eat and to allow them to rest on Shabbat.

PRACTICAL EXERCISES

Now that you have been exposed to many different mitzvahs that are part of your everyday life, how can you apply them? It helps to keep a journal or log of your activities. Write down what you did this morning. Then think of the mitzvah that fits with the action. Sometimes one action can encompass several different mitzvahs at the same time. Here is an example:

Woke up, said *Modah Ani*, washed hands (mitzvah of prayer). Got kids ready, fed and on the bus (mitzvah of emulating God, taking care of body, teaching Torah). Fed dogs (mitzvah). Drank my tea (mitzvah of saying blessing). Walked the dogs (another mitzvah). Called my mom (mitzvah, mitzvah mitzvah!!!) And it's only 8:15!!

PRACTICAL EXERCISES

The more familiar you get with the mitzvahs, the easier it is to apply them. The next step is applying them real time. So then you are doing your daily activities with an awareness of God. This should make what you're doing feel important and valuable.

What if it doesn't? I have to admit there are times when I lose sight of all of this mitzvah stuff. I get cranky, angry, and frustrated and there are times when I feel unproductive, unappreciated and undone. This like everything else in life is temporary and fleeting. The mood changes, the doorbell rings, a good song comes on the radio and you're back on track. Remember just like God commands you to love your neighbor, don't forget to love yourself. Just as you are commanded to judge others favorably, cut yourself some slack. Every day is an opportunity to start fresh. God is constantly giving us new chances to connect and elevate ourselves, even during the most seemingly trivial tasks.

The mitzvahs you do in your life are eternal. No one can do them like you and no one can take them from you. So wherever you go today and whatever you do, grab a mitzvah on the way. Grab as many as you can. And don't forget the dry cleaning!!

THANKS

With gratitude to Hashem for giving me the strength and skills to complete this project. Thank you to my parents, Marilyn and Irv Sultz who have whole heartedly embraced my journey. To Rabbi Yaakov and Faygie Bienenfeld who provide vibrant, living examples of Torah observance. To Esther Baila Schwarz for her passionate teachings. To Nico Bishop whose art direction and design made this book look good. And to my kind and patient and wise friends; you know who you are.

ONLINE RESOURCES

Here are several websites that I have found to be very helpful on my Jewish journey. For a complete listing of all 613 mitzvot go to Chabad.org

Chabad.org (candlelighting times, general info)

Aish.com (great articles and family parsha)

MyJewishlearning.com (great for kids)

Naaleh.com (great free classes)

ONLINE RESOURCES

Englishtorahtapes.com (more great free classes)

Jewishvirtuallibrary.org

Torah.org

MITZVAHS IN THIS BOOK

To know that God exists (Exodus 20:2)

Not to blaspheme (Exodus 22:27)

To hallow God's name (Leviticus 22:32)

Not to profane God's name (Leviticus 22:32)

To know that God is One, a complete Unity (Deuteronomy 6:4)

To love God (Deuteronomy 6:5)

To fear God reverently (Deuteronomy 6:13; 10:20)

To imitate His good and upright ways (Deuteronomy 28:9)

To learn Torah and to teach it (Deuteronomy 6:7)

To pray to (serve) God (Exodus 23:25; Deuteronomy 6:13)

To read the Shema in the morning and at night (Deuteronomy 6:7)

Not to eat or drink to excess (Deuteronomy 21:20)

To recite grace after meals (Deuteronomy 8:10)

To love all human beings who are of the covenant (Leviticus 19:18)

To love the stranger (Deuteronomy 10:19)

Not to stand by idly when a human life is in danger (Leviticus 19:16).

Not to wrong any one in speech (Leviticus 25:17)

Not to wrong the stranger in speech (Exodus 22:20)

Not to carry tales (Leviticus 19:16)

Not to have hatred in one's heart (Leviticus 19:17)

Not to take revenge (Leviticus 19:18)

Not to bear a grudge (Leviticus 19:18)

Not to put any Jew to shame (Leviticus 19:17)

Not to curse any other Israelite (Leviticus 19:14)

Not to make an idol (even for others) to worship (Exodus 20:4)

Not to worship idols (Exodus 20:5)

Not to bow down to an idol (Exodus 20:5)

Not to give occasion to the simple-minded to stumble on the road (Leviticus 19:14)

Not to refrain from maintaining a poor man and giving him what he needs (Deuteronomy 15:7).

To give charity according to one's means (Deuteronomy 15:11)

Not to wrong the stranger in buying or selling (Exodus 22:20

To honor father and mother (Exodus 20:12)

Not to curse a father or mother (Exodus 21:17)

To reverently fear mother and father (Leviticus 19:3)

To honor the old and the wise (Leviticus 19:32)

Not to delay payment of a hired man's wages (Leviticus 19:13)

That a man should fulfill whatever he has uttered (Deuteronomy 23:24)

Not to swear needlessly (Exodus 20:7)

To return lost property (Deuteronomy 22:1)

Not to pretend not to have seen lost property, to avoid the obligation to return it (Deuteronomy 22:3)

Not to covet what belongs to another (Exodus 20:14)

Not to crave something that belongs to another (Deuteronomy 5:18)

To sanctify Shabbat (Exodus 20:8)

Not to do work on Shabbat (Exodus 20:10)

To rest on Shabbat (Exodus 23:12; 34:21)

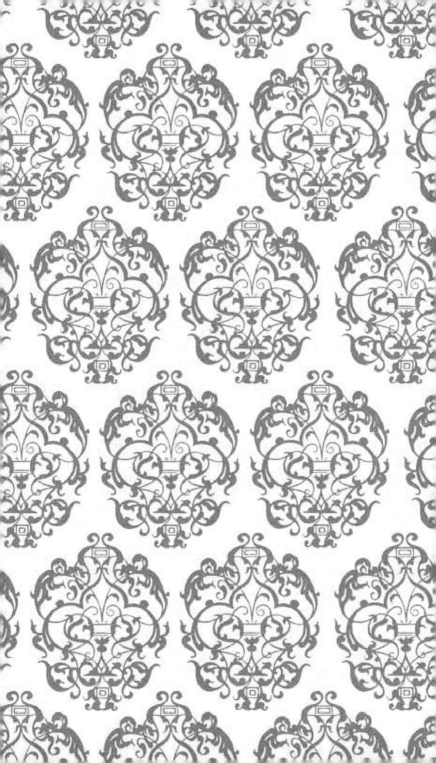